FEARLESS

★ THE STORY OF ★

RACING LEGEND

★ LOUISE SMITH ★

BARB ROSENSTOCK
ILLUSTRATED BY SCOTT DAWSON

DUTTON CHILDREN'S BOOKS ★ An imprint of Penguin Group (USA) Inc.

★ ★ ★

"I WON A LOT, CRASHED A LOT, AND BROKE JUST ABOUT EVERY BONE IN MY BODY, BUT I GAVE IT EVERYTHING I HAD."
—*LOUISE SMITH* (1916–2006)

A LEGACY IS SOMETHING THAT PASSES FROM ONE GENERATION to the next . . . a family business . . . money . . . children. Louise Smith never had her own children, and she passed on without a bit of extra money. Yet the legend of the woman who dared to drive with the men is still told. Her legacy lives on in those stories and in the free spirits of all the brave, wild girls yet to come. That legacy is the gift of independence, a heart full of courage, and the chance to prove that being a girl should never stop anyone from going anywhere they want . . . as far and as fast as they can.

To Mom and Dad for a good beginning, and to Marc
for the rest of the story.
—B.R.

To my parents, Win and Sandy Dawson.
Thanks for all your love and encouragement.
—S.D.

DUTTON CHILDREN'S BOOKS • *A division of Penguin Young Readers Group*

Published by the Penguin Group

Penguin Group (USA) Inc., 375 Hudson Street, New York, New York 10014, U.S.A. • Penguin Group (Canada), 90 Eglinton Avenue East, Suite 700, Toronto, Ontario M4P 2Y3, Canada (a division of Pearson Penguin Canada Inc.) • Penguin Books Ltd, 80 Strand, London WC2R 0RL, England • Penguin Ireland, 25 St Stephen's Green, Dublin 2, Ireland (a division of Penguin Books Ltd) • Penguin Group (Australia), 250 Camberwell Road, Camberwell, Victoria 3124, Australia (a division of Pearson Australia Group Pty Ltd) • Penguin Books India Pvt Ltd, 11 Community Centre, Panchsheel Park, New Delhi—110 017, India • Penguin Group (NZ), 67 Apollo Drive, Rosedale, North Shore 0632, New Zealand (a division of Pearson New Zealand Ltd) • Penguin Books (South Africa) (Pty) Ltd, 24 Sturdee Avenue, Rosebank, Johannesburg 2196, South Africa • Penguin Books Ltd, Registered Offices: 80 Strand, London WC2R 0RL, England

CIP Data is available.

Published in the United States by Dutton Children's Books, a division of Penguin Young Readers Group
345 Hudson Street, New York, New York 10014 • www.penguin.com/youngreaders

Designed by Jason Henry

Manufactured in China • First Edition
ISBN: 978-0-525-42173-3 • 10 9 8 7 6 5 4 3 2 1

Photo on page 32 used with the kind permission of Lib Owens.

IN THOSE DAYS IT WAS PRETTY TOUGH TO BE A GIRL.

You had to follow the rules. You couldn't speak your mind. You had to ask permission.

There were games you couldn't play and clubs you couldn't join. You weren't allowed at the best schools. You were supposed to stay clean, quiet, and obedient.

Louise was a girl of those times, but she didn't play by the rules. Most of the time, she did exactly as she pleased.

Which is how she found her seven-year-old self on a bumpy farm road, behind the wheel of her daddy's automobile.

Louise had watched the boys drive a hundred times. She revved the engine. Felt it rumble in her chest. She smashed down the gas pedal . . .

and left those boys in the dust!
FAST! FASTER! FLYING!
FREE!
Louise felt that she was finally going fast enough to get somewhere.

Until she hit the chicken coop.

When the boys caught up, they found splinters of wood on the seats, chicken feathers thick in the air, and Louise . . .

still hanging onto the wheel, laughing like crazy.
She never did ask how to stop.

As she grew up, Louise did what girls in her town were supposed to do. She worked at the cotton mill. She got married. Her husband, Noah Smith, owned a junkyard that sold car parts. She helped run the business.

Louise tried, but she couldn't settle down. She hopped from job to job—nurse, lifeguard, beautician. She always spoke her mind. She didn't follow the rules.

Alone on the roads late at night, Louise would drive.
FAST! FASTER! FLYING!
FREE!

She drove until she felt that she was finally going fast enough to get somewhere—even if she always wound up right back home.

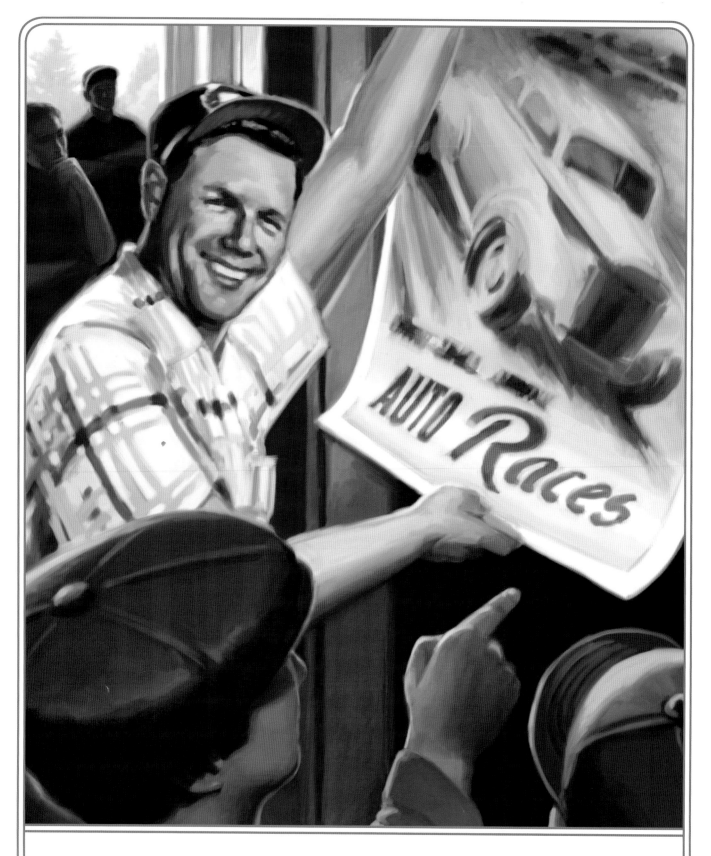

Until the day "Big Bill" France came to town.

Big Bill promoted auto races. He brought people to the track to see this new sport. He went looking for a girl who could drive in a race as a gimmick, a joke.

Everyone knew girls couldn't really race cars.
He found Louise.
"The craziest woman we know," said the neighbors.

Which is how Louise, who had never even seen a car race before, found herself on a hot, dirt track, behind the wheel of a borrowed race car, in front of hundreds of people in her hometown, one wild, summer night.

They told her the rules:

Stay on the track. Green means GO. Red means STOP.
Louise revved the engine. Felt it rumble in her chest.
A flag waved.

GREEN. GO!

She smashed down the gas pedal and left those boys in the dust!
FAST! FASTER! FLYING!
FREE!
Around and around. Ten times. Twenty times. Thirty times.
A checkered flag waved. The race was over.
Louise kept going.

Louise didn't know what the checkered flag meant. She would not stop. When someone remembered to wave a *red* flag, Louise pulled in. She'd come in third, beating a pack of experienced men. That day the crowd learned women could race.
Louise learned she could be one of the best.

Noah worried. Racing was tough. Tough for men. *Too* tough for a woman. He saw wrecked cars every day. He didn't want Louise hurt; he told her never to race again.

Louise found a way to do exactly as she pleased.

She told Noah she was headed south for a little vacation. She drove his new car to Daytona to watch the best drivers in the country race on the beach.

Once she got there, Louise just had to see if she was good enough.

Which is how she found herself taping a number 94 on the side of Noah's car, covering the headlights to save them from flying sand, and tucking her hair into a small, white racing helmet.

Some of the male drivers yelled insults at Louise.

"Get out of my way, woman!" "Crazy fool!" "Think you're pretty tough?"

Nervously, Louise tied herself to the seat with a piece of rope. The ocean waves roared on one side of the track and a crowd of thousands roared on the other. Louise revved the engine. Felt it rumble in her chest.

GO!

She smashed down the gas pedal and left those boys in the dust!
FAST! FASTER! FLYING!
FREE!
Sand and muck churned onto the windshield from the cars ahead.
Louise squinted to see through the mess. Sliding through a turn,
Louise hit a rut. Her car bounced in the air and flipped. She got the
car turned over, climbed back in, and kept going. She didn't win.
But she finished. She would not stop.

Noah's car was so smashed that Louise had to take the bus home.
"Where's my car?" asked Noah.
"Oh, that ol' thing broke down in Georgia," fibbed Louise.
Noah held up the newspaper: LOUISE SMITH WRECKS CAR AT DAYTONA
Noah loved Louise and Louise loved racing. Noah gave in. He helped Louise find decent cars and mechanics. But he never, ever watched her race.

Louise traveled with a gang of rowdy men storming tracks from Canada to Alabama. They called her the "Good ol' Gal." They raced for a hundred dollars if they won and got nothing if they didn't. It was a tough life. Drivers fought, slept in their cars, and split a hot dog or a can of sardines for dinner.

Louise earned respect. She drove tough. She drove to win.

Still, in every town, there were men who didn't want her on the track. Louise learned to protect herself.

If a driver gave her trouble,

SWOOSH, she cut him off by broadsiding a turn;

CRUNCH, she sent his car into the wall; or best of all
VA-VROOM, she beat him to the finish line.
FAST! FASTER! FLYING!
FREE!

Louise was fearless. She would not stop. She either won or she wrecked. Mostly, she wrecked. Once she wound up sitting on the roof of her car in a lake. Another time she zoomed through a wooden fence only to speed right back onto the track—with feed bags flapping off her windshield!

A few times she was badly hurt; one airborne crash into a stand of trees almost killed her.

But on most nights, Louise stepped out of her wrecked car with a big, dimpled smile on her face. She posed for photographers. Racing fans adored her.

Louise drove for eleven years. She won thirty-eight times. She was the first woman elected to the International Motorsports Hall of Fame—forty-three years after she stopped racing.

As Louise got old, walking got harder, but driving never did. Wearing rhinestone bifocals, sparkly earrings, and hair piled high on her head, Louise pushed her sedan to the limit,

60 . . . 70 . . . 80 miles an hour. Yep, the old lady could still drive fast enough to go anywhere she wanted.

FAST! FASTER! FLYING! FREE!

FEARLESS!

★ AUTHOR'S NOTE ★

THERE ARE HUNDREDS OF LOUISE SMITH STORIES, none of them told the same way twice. When she was alive, Louise also told stories, and even her own versions changed depending on the audience. The facts of Louise's life and the early history of stock-car racing are true; however, sometimes legends can be hard to prove.

Louise started driving stock cars in the days before NASCAR. In fact it was "Big Bill" France who founded NASCAR in 1948, just a few years after discovering Louise in Greenville, South Carolina. The car races down Daytona Beach and around Highway A1A later became the world famous Daytona 500.

In the early days, drivers were paid next to nothing. They were small town men who drove for the love of fast cars, or to be famous. Louise drove with legendary NASCAR drivers Buck Baker, Glenn "Fireball" Roberts, Curtis Turner, Buddy Shuman, and the Flock Brothers.

Professional auto racing is a tough way to make a living. In the 1940s and 1950s, it was even tougher than it is today. Cars were stripped down inside to the bare metal before the races. Roll bars, seat belts, and fire protection were not required. The lightweight driving helmets had less head protection than a bike helmet does today. Drivers wore their street clothes, in Louise's case, pedal pushers, sneakers, and a cotton shirt. Many a night ended with a driver seriously hurt, burned, or killed. At the Occoneechee Speedway in 1950, Louise had a nearly fatal crash into some trees. It took rescuers almost an hour to cut her out of the wreck with a blowtorch. She suffered a concussion, broken bones, and needed four pins and forty-eight stitches to put her left knee back together. She drove again as soon as she could.

Louise was not the only woman at the track on those wild summer nights, but there were very few. Other well-known female drivers of the time were Ethel Mobley, sister of the Flock Brothers, and Sara Christian, wife of driver Frank Christian, who in 1949 became the first woman to compete in a NASCAR event.

From the mid-1950s until the mid-1970s, women were banned from the track on the grounds that it was too dangerous for them. Some still raced in ladies races at small tracks around the country, but usually women were allowed to participate only as beauty queens. It wasn't until much later that Janet Guthrie, Patty Moise, Shirley Muldowney, Shawna Robinson, Erin Crocker, Danica Patrick and others continued the tradition of women as professional race drivers.

THANKS TO the Living Legends of Auto Racing members for the interviews and stories, especially: H. L. "Peanut" Turman, Tommy Gooch, J. B. Day, Yolanda Sheridan, Lois Tyler, Vicki Wood, and Mr. Ray Fox Sr. Thanks also to Buz McKim, NASCAR historian, International Speed Corporation Archive staff; Suzanne Heddy, Halifax Historical Museum; Colleen Koebel, Cook Memorial Library; Durham Hunt IV, Greenville Public Library; Betty Carlan, International Motorsports Hall of Fame; and Lib Owens.

Other sources include: Atwell, Cheryl, ed., *Welcome to the Racing Zone*, Halifax Historical Museum, Jan. 2003. Biddle, Joe, *The Lady Called Lou, Daytona Beach News Journal*, 7/1/79. Causey, Frances W., Warner, John W. IV, et al., *The Golden Era of NASCAR*, Stonebridge Productions, 2005. Deitsch, Richard, *Flashback, Louise Smith, 82, Stock Racing Pioneer*, SI for Women, 8/6/99. Fant, Reese, *Greenville's own stock car veteran, Greenville News*, 10/6/91. Feilden, Greg, *High Speed at Low Tide*, Garfield Press, 1993. Golenbock, Peter, *NASCAR Confidential*, MBI Publishing, 2004. Holder, Bill, *A NASCAR Pioneer*, pub. unknown, collection of Wm. Van Wert. Hunt, Sandra, *There'll Never Be Another Louise Smith*, pub. unknown, International Motorsports Hall of Fame. Parente, Audrey, Koblas, Jack, *Women of Speed*, Trackside, 4/28–5/11/95. Staff writers, *Louise Smith, Clardy Wreck Cars, Greenville Piedmont*, 7/11/49. Williams, Deb, *Louise Smith*, pub. unknown, ISC archive.